I0816705

OUTDOOR ADVENTURES and SPORTS

KAYAKING

James De Medeiros

AV2

www.openlightbox.com

Step 1
Go to **www.openlightbox.com**

Step 2
Enter this unique code
ZDWTL0LY4

Step 3
Explore your interactive eBook!

AV2 is optimized for use on any device

Your interactive eBook comes with...

Contents
Browse a live contents page to easily navigate through resources

Audio
Listen to sections of the book read aloud

Videos
Watch informative video clips

Weblinks
Gain additional information for research

Slideshows
View images and captions

Try This!
Complete activities and hands-on experiments

Key Words
Study vocabulary, and complete a matching word activity

Quizzes
Test your knowledge

Share
Share titles within your Learning Management System (LMS) or Library Circulation System

Citation
Create bibliographical references following the Chicago Manual of Style

This title is part of our AV2 digital subscription

1-Year K–5 Subscription
ISBN 978-1-7911-3320-7

Access hundreds of AV2 titles with our digital subscription.
Sign up for a FREE trial at **www.openlightbox.com/trial**

OUTDOOR ADVENTURES and SPORTS

KAYAKING

CONTENTS

All About Kayaking

A kayak is a small, light boat. It has a single opening in the center called a cockpit. This is where kayakers sit. They can move and steer the kayak with a double-bladed paddle.

The Inuit are a group of Native Americans who live in the far north. They made the first kayaks from wooden frames and animal skins. They had two types of kayaks. One was wide and had space to store items. The other kayak was long and sleek. The shape of this kayak helped the kayaker move more quickly through the water.

Over time, the design of the kayak changed. People began making kayaks out of different materials. **Synthetic** material replaced animal skins. In the 1950s, **fiberglass** started to be used instead of wooden frames. In the 1980s, fiberglass frames were replaced by plastic frames. All of these changes were made to improve kayaking as a sport.

Competitive kayaking began in 1873. That year, the Royal Canoe Club of Great Britain began holding kayak races. Today, people around the world kayak for fun and for sport.

Changes Throughout the Years

PAST	PRESENT
Kayaks were used for hunting.	People kayak for fun or for competition.
Kayaks were made out of wood and animal skins.	Kayaks are made out of plastic or fiberglass.
The Inuit wore warm clothing while kayaking.	In cool climates, kayakers wear a wet suit.
People did not usually wear safety gear while kayaking.	Most kayakers wear a vest that keeps them afloat.

Getting Started

Kayaking can be a dangerous sport. It is important to be prepared with the proper equipment, including safety gear. The most important piece of equipment is the kayak. There are many different types of kayaks, such as touring kayaks, folding kayaks, inflatable kayaks, and rigid kayaks.

Folding kayaks are similar to Inuit kayaks. They are made by placing fabric over a light wooden or aluminum frame. Folding kayaks can be taken apart and folded for storage. They are as sturdy as regular kayaks.

Touring kayaks are used for long-distance trips or for kayaking at sea. They are larger than many other types of kayaks. This makes them less likely to tip or turn over. Touring kayaks are made from plastic or fiberglass. They may have a place to store equipment.

Inflatable kayaks float better than many other types of kayaks. They are less likely to tip over. This is because they are filled with air. When not in use, the air can be removed from an inflatable kayak.

1 Double-bladed kayak paddles come in different lengths and widths. A long paddle is suited for a long kayak or tall person. A shorter paddle is suited for a shorter kayak or smaller person.

2 Helmets protect kayakers from hitting their head on objects in the water, such as rocks and logs.

3 A skirt is a piece of fabric that fits around a kayaker's waist. It attaches to the edge of the cockpit. Skirts prevent water from filling the kayak and causing it to sink.

Rigid kayaks can absorb the impact of rocks. This makes them popular for trips down fast-moving rivers with large rocks.

4 Wet suits keep kayakers warm in cold water. A wet suit absorbs water. Then, the kayaker's body heat warms up the water that the wet suit absorbs. This creates a warm layer between the kayaker and the cold water.

5 Most experienced kayakers prefer a tight cockpit space. Beginners learn better with a bigger cockpit. There are multiple passenger kayaks for families who like to kayak together. Most kayaks have a small storage space behind the seat.

6 A personal flotation device is a jacket or vest that a kayaker wears in the water to keep afloat.

Kayaking Basics

There are many ways to paddle a kayak. As a beginner, the most important techniques are the forward, sweep, and brace strokes. The forward stroke helps the kayaker move forward. He or she places the right side of the paddle in the water near the front of the kayak and pulls the blade toward the back of the boat. Then, the kayaker places the left side of the paddle in the water and pulls back.

Sweep strokes can turn the kayak forward or backward. This is done by placing the paddle in the water near the front of the kayak. The kayaker then sweeps the paddle out to the side and back, forming an arc in the water.

Brace strokes are especially important for beginners. Bracing keeps kayaks from tipping over. The simplest form of bracing is to keep one paddle blade underwater. High and low bracing requires kayakers to push the blade of their paddle against the flow of water. This is done by leaning forward.

It is important for beginners to learn paddling techniques in calm waters.

Even if a kayaker knows how to brace, kayaks can still tip over, leaving the kayaker upside down. To turn the kayak right side up, the kayaker must be able to roll the kayak. A roll is achieved when the kayaker, still in the kayak, moves his or her hips so that the body is twisted sideways. At this point, the kayaker lifts the paddle out of the water, keeping it **parallel** to the kayak. Then, the kayaker sweeps the right paddle blade away from the kayak and into the water. Holding the left elbow close to the body, the kayaker snaps his or her back into a straight position while sweeping, turning the kayak right side up.

Wrapping reflective tape around a paddle can prove useful. If the paddle gets lost in a fast flowing river, the reflective tape will make it easier to find.

Rolling a kayak takes strength, skill, and experience. This is an important skill to know before kayaking in challenging waters.

Kayaking Levels

Whitewater, or river, kayaking is an **extreme sport**. It requires skill and experience. There are six levels, or classes, of difficulty for this sport. Beginners often start in the first two classes. Class One is the easiest. At this level, the water moves quickly but without any waves or **obstructions**. If the kayak rolls or tips and the kayaker falls out, the water is mild. It is easy to swim to shore. Class Two is similar to Class One, but there may be rocks in the water and slightly bigger waves.

Class Three is for experienced kayakers. It has big waves and narrow paths. Class Four has powerful waves that make paddling more difficult. Inexperienced kayakers should avoid these conditions.

Class Five is especially difficult and is for experts only. Rescues are difficult to perform on Class Five or higher **rapids**. These routes are known for violent and obstructed paths with very fast-flowing water.

Class Six is known for extremely dangerous conditions. It is strongly advised to avoid Class Six rapids. They are dangerous and highly unpredictable. Even expert kayakers risk serious injury by trying Class Six rapids.

River conditions can change in difficulty during different seasons. It is important to check the river conditions before each kayaking trip.

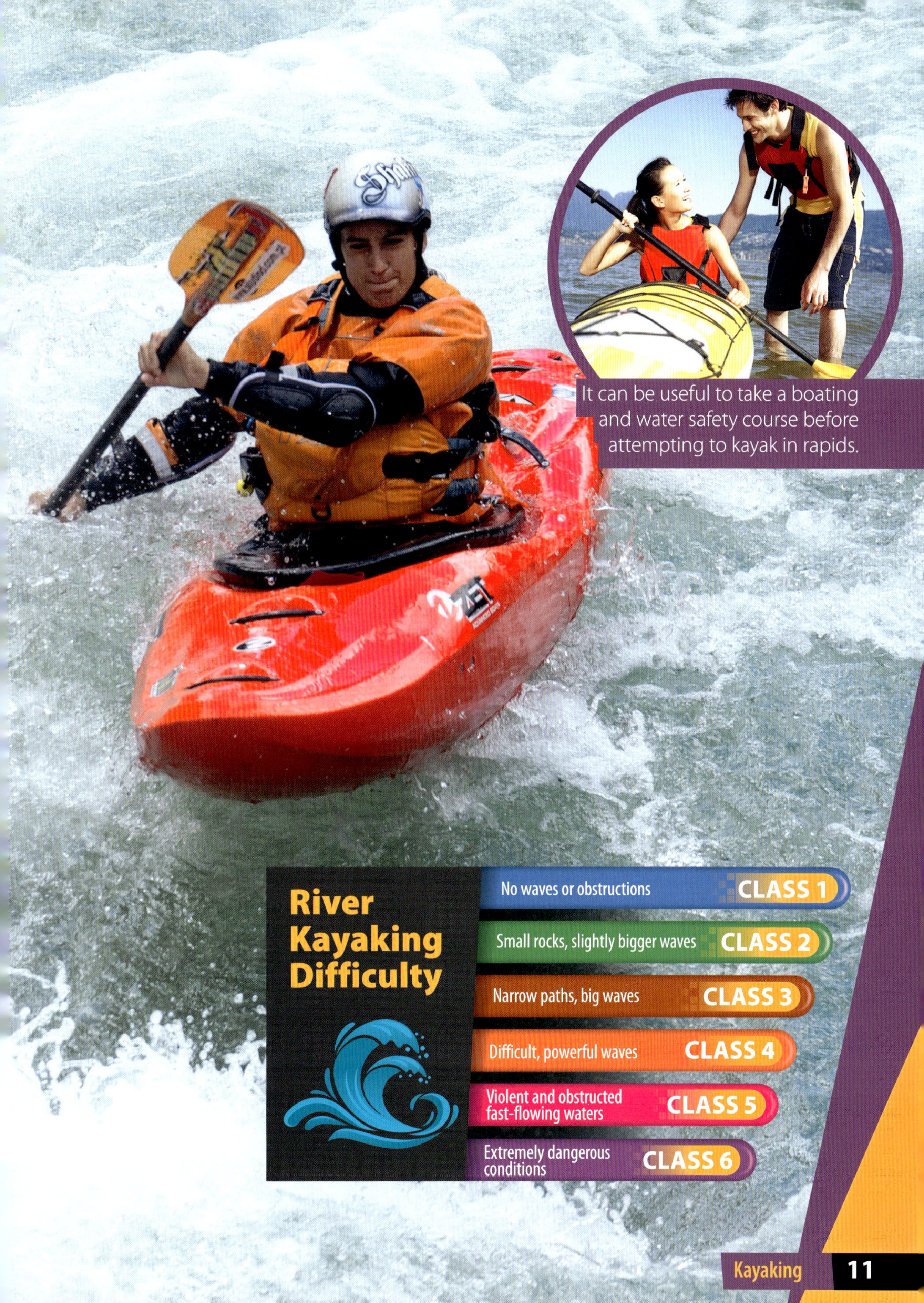

It can be useful to take a boating and water safety course before attempting to kayak in rapids.

River Kayaking Difficulty

Description	Class
No waves or obstructions	CLASS 1
Small rocks, slightly bigger waves	CLASS 2
Narrow paths, big waves	CLASS 3
Difficult, powerful waves	CLASS 4
Violent and obstructed fast-flowing waters	CLASS 5
Extremely dangerous conditions	CLASS 6

Staying Safe

Kayaking can be dangerous because it is hard to predict what might happen in rapids. With proper training and experience, most people learn to read the rapids for signs of danger so they can plan fun, safe trips.

To stay safe, kayakers must remain calm. They should know how to react under different circumstances, and they should build up their physical conditioning to prepare for long journeys. Kayakers who have never paddled for more than two hours at one time should not go on a four-hour trip. They cannot take breaks on the water. The only time kayakers can rest is when they have returned to shore.

Kayakers should always check weather reports before going on a trip. It is dangerous to kayak during a storm. Waves and wind can change a Class Three rapid to a Class Six. Another risk is extreme cold. Cool temperatures and wet clothing increase the risk of **hypothermia**.

All kayakers should learn rescue skills. Accidents can happen at any time, and people should always be prepared to help themselves and anyone else in need of assistance on the water. Rescue skills include **cardiopulmonary resuscitation (CPR)** and basic first aid. Kayakers should also know kayaking signals, such as stop, help, and all is clear. To signal stop, kayakers stretch both arms out from their sides to form a horizontal line. They may also signal stop by holding a paddle above their heads in a horizontal line. Help is signaled by waving a paddle, helmet, or life vest above the head. To let others know all is clear ahead, kayakers hold one arm or a paddle straight up, high above their heads.

#2 Kayaking Tip
Treat hypothermia by removing all wet clothing. Put on warm, dry clothing. Cut a hole for your head in a garbage bag, and wear the bag like a shirt. This will help reduce heat loss.
One of the most important kayaking abilities is matching one's skill level to the difficulty of the rapids.
Rescue Signals
Help
Stop
All Is Clear

Explore the Outdoors

There are many outdoor activities that can be enjoyed on the water in addition to kayaking. Some of these activities include whitewater rafting, water skiing, fishing, and canoeing.

Whitewater Rafting

In whitewater rafting, people travel down river rapids. The rafts are inflatable rubber boats. Often, they are steered by a professional guide who sits at the back of the raft. Many people can fit in a raft. They help the guide steer the raft.

Water Skiing

Water skiing was invented in 1922 by an 18-year-old boy named Ralph Samuelson. To water ski, the skiers have one or two skis attached to their feet, and they are pulled behind a boat. People who become very good at water skiing can take part in competitions that are held around the world.

Canoeing

Though they look like kayaks, canoes are quite different. A canoe does not have a skirt, and most canoes are built to fit more than one person. Unlike kayak paddles, canoe paddles only have a blade at one end. Most people only use canoes on calm waters with few or small waves.

Fishing

Beneath the surface of rivers, lakes, and oceans are many types of life, including fish. **Recreational** fishers use a fishing rod, line, hook, and **bait** to catch fish. Fishing can be done from the shore, from a boat, or from a kayak. Most types of fishing are not physically demanding. People of any fitness level can fish. However, fishers do need patience to enjoy this pastime.

Kayaking Around the World

There are many places in the world where people can kayak. The best places to kayak depend on what a kayaker enjoys the most. Some places have challenging Class Six rapids. Others have beautiful natural areas. The following are a few of the places to kayak around the world.

1 Everglades National Park, United States

The Everglades offers kayakers the opportunity to explore beautiful and varied landscapes, including freshwater marshes, mangrove forests, and the open waters of Florida Bay.

2 Cyclades Islands, Greece

With more than 30 islands, including beautiful Santorini, kayakers can enjoy the warm climate while trying to spot sea life in the clear water.

3 Rock Islands, Palau

Kayakers and sport divers enjoy these 445 tiny limestone islands, which are famous for their sea caves, sunken ships, and even sunken airplanes.

4 Great Barrier Reef, Australia

The largest coral **barrier reef** in the world offers kayakers the chance to see almost 1,500 kinds of fish, 16 species of sea snakes, and 215 varieties of birds.

Join the Club

There are many kayaking clubs around the world. No matter where a person lives, there is likely a kayaking club nearby. California alone has more than 15 kayaking clubs.

Competitive kayaking is becoming more popular around the world. At the Summer Olympic Games, there are kayaking competitions for both men and women. Events include whitewater and flat water races. The gold medal in each competition is won by the person with the fastest time. Medals are also given for second and third place.

Many smaller competitions take place throughout the world as well. It is at these local events that kayakers sharpen their skills. These competitions help decide which kayakers will represent their countries at the Olympic Games and world championships.

Kayaking has been an Olympic sport since 1936.

Nonprofit clubs such as the American Canoe Association organize many kayaking events each year and help people meet other kayakers.

Healthy Habits

Kayakers must stay fit. One of the best ways to keep in shape is to eat healthy foods. Balanced meals of grains, fruits, vegetables, dairy products, and protein will give kayakers more energy.

Grains include anything made from wheat or rice, such as bread, cereal, and pasta. All fruits and vegetables are healthy. Most nutritionists recommend eating five to ten servings of fruits or vegetables a day. A serving can be half a cup of juice or a piece of medium-sized fruit, such as a banana. People should choose low-fat dairy products, such as skim milk, low-fat cheese, or yogurt. Lean meats, such as fish or chicken, are also part of a healthy diet.

Dry Land Stretches

The following exercises stretch the body in the three directions a person can move in a kayak. Try holding each stretch for 15 to 20 seconds, and repeat three times on each side.

"C" STRETCH
Sit on the floor, and raise your arms above your head. Lean to the side.

TORSO TWIST
Sitting down, twist your chest and shoulders while keeping your lower body in place.

LEG STRETCH
Lie on your back, lifting one leg straight up in the air. Grasp the leg with your hands and pull.

Kayakers need energy, flexibility, and strength to paddle. Whether people want to be competitive or recreational kayakers, the more strength they have, the easier the activity will be. Flexibility allows kayakers to twist their upper body. Twisting is an essential movement for the sport. Kayakers must be able to twist in order to perform a roll that will flip upside down kayaks right side up.

Stretching before kayaking can help prevent injuries.

The best time to go kayaking is when the wind is calm and the water is still. However, if the wind or waves pick up, kayakers should head to shore before it is unsafe to be on the water.

Quiz

1. Where does a kayaker sit?
2. What piece of equipment is used to steer the kayak?
3. How many classes of rapids are there?
4. What are the three main kayaking strokes?
5. What year did kayaking become an Olympic sport?
6. Who designed the first two types of kayaks?

Answers

1. A kayaker sits in the middle of the boat in an area called the cockpit. **2.** The kayaker uses the paddle to move the kayak in any direction. **3.** There are six classes of rapids. **4.** The three main kayaking strokes are the forward, sweep, and brace strokes. **5.** Kayaking became an Olympic sport in 1936. **6.** The Inuit designed the first two types of kayaks.

Key Words

bait: food used to catch fish
barrier reef: a coral reef that runs along a shoreline but is separated from the shore by water
cardiopulmonary resuscitation (CPR): a life-saving technique that combines rescue breathing with chest compressions; used when a person stops breathing and his or her heart stops beating
extreme sport: difficult or dangerous physical activity
fiberglass: a strong material made from fine threads of glass
hypothermia: a dangerous loss of body heat caused by extremely cold weather
obstructions: objects in the water that a kayaker might hit, such as rocks and tree branches
parallel: being the same distance apart at all points
rapids: shallow parts of rivers where rocks are exposed and fast-moving water creates waves
recreational: something done for fun or relaxation, such as hobbies, games, and sports
synthetic: made by people; not natural

Index

Get the best of both worlds.

AV2 bridges the gap between print and digital.

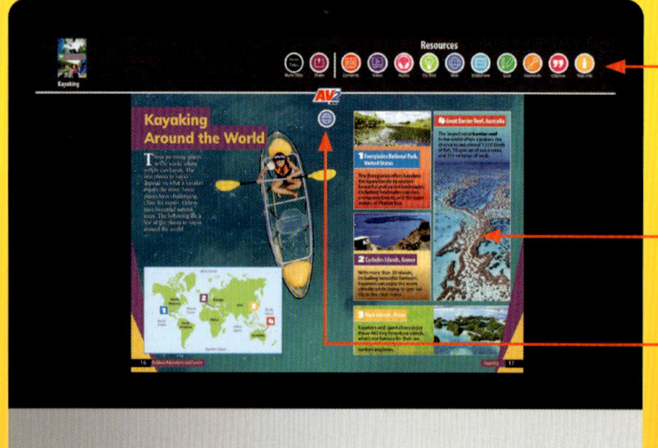

The expandable resources toolbar enables quick access to content including **videos**, **audio**, **activities**, **weblinks**, **slideshows**, **quizzes**, and **key words**.

Animated videos make static images come alive.

Resource icons on each page help readers to further **explore key concepts**.

Published by Lightbox Learning Inc.
276 5th Avenue, Suite 704 #917
New York, NY 10001
Website: www.openlightbox.com

Library of Congress Cataloging-in-Publication Data

Names: De Medeiros, James, 1975- author.
Title: Kayaking / James De Medeiros.
Other titles: Kayaking (Outdoor adventures and sports)
Description: New York, NY : Lightbox Learning Inc., [2023] | Series: Outdoor adventures and sports | Includes index. | Audience: Grades 4-6
Identifiers: LCCN 2022024427 (print) | LCCN 2022024428 (ebook) | ISBN 9781791147457 (library binding) | ISBN 9781791147464 (paperback) | ISBN 9781791147471
Subjects: LCSH: Kayaking--Juvenile literature.
Classification: LCC GV784.3 .D46 2023 (print) | LCC GV784.3 (ebook) | DDC 797.122/4--dc23/eng/20220527
LC record available at https://lccn.loc.gov/2022024427
LC ebook record available at https://lccn.loc.gov/2022024428

Printed in Guangzhou, China
1 2 3 4 5 6 7 8 9 0 26 25 24 23 22

062022
101121

Project Coordinator Priyanka Das
Designer Terry Paulhus

Photo Credits
Every reasonable effort has been made to trace ownership and to obtain permission to reprint copyright material. The publisher would be pleased to have any errors or omissions brought to its attention so that they may be corrected in subsequent printings. The publisher acknowledges Getty Images and Shutterstock as its primary image suppliers for this title.